Bold and Brilliant
Women at the Intersection of Blockchain & AI

Cassandra Diane Ford

Table of Contents

1. Introduction . . . 2
2. Trailblazers: Women Leading Technological Revolution . . . 3
   2.1. The Forerunners: Setting Precedents in Tech . . . 3
   2.2. Modern Masters: Contemporary Tech Leaders . . . 3
   2.3. Pioneers of the New: Blockchain and AI . . . 4
   2.4. Beating Barriers: Women of Resilience . . . 4
   2.5. In the Limelight: Women Making Global Impact . . . 5
3. Humble Beginnings: Early Encounters with Technology . . . 6
   3.1. The Spark Ignites . . . 6
   3.2. Awakening a Lifelong Passion . . . 7
   3.3. The Journey into the Future . . . 7
4. Coding the Future: A Deep Dive into Blockchain . . . 9
   4.1. The Fundamentals of Blockchain . . . 9
   4.2. Women in Blockchain . . . 10
   4.3. Pathbreakers and their Contributions . . . 11
   4.4. The Advancements and Challenges . . . 11
   4.5. The Vision of the Future . . . 12
5. Taking on AI: Decoding the New Intelligence . . . 14
   5.1. Machine Learning: Understanding AI's Brainchild . . . 14
   5.2. The Deep Learning Revolution . . . 15
   5.3. Conversational AI: Resetting Communication Paradigms . . . 15
   5.4. AI and Ethics: Untangling the Complex Web . . . 16
6. Mind the Gap: Overcoming Gender Divide in Tech . . . 17
   6.1. The Historical Tapestry of Women in Tech . . . 17
   6.2. The Present Predicament: Underrepresentation and Stereotyping . . . 18
   6.3. Moving the Needle: Inspiring Initiatives and Structural Changes . . . 18

- 6.4. Overcoming Mitigations: Tackling Imposter Syndrome and Gender Bias … 19
- 6.5. Visions for the Future: Empowering the Next Generation … 19
- 7. Leading Lights: Profiles of Female Tech Giants … 21
  - 7.1. The First Adventurer: Ada Lovelace … 21
  - 7.2. Grace Hopper: The Debugging Whiz … 21
  - 7.3. Radia Perlman: The Internet's Unsung Heroine … 22
  - 7.4. Sheryl Sandberg: From Google to Facebook … 22
  - 7.5. Ginni Rometty: Traversing the IBM Frontier … 22
  - 7.6. Susan Wojcicki: YouTube's Visionary Leader … 23
  - 7.7. Blockchain and AI Pioneers: Overcoming the Uncanny Valley … 23
- 8. Navigating Challenges: Tales of Grit and Perseverance … 25
  - 8.1. Battling Bias: Encountering the Prejudiced Mindset … 25
  - 8.2. Defying Odds: Rising Above Personal Battles … 26
  - 8.3. Surmounting Structural Barriers: Fighting the System … 26
  - 8.4. The Currency of Courage: Unmasking Bravery and Persistence … 27
- 9. WiT: Women in Tech's Impact on Global Economy … 28
  - 9.1. Transforming Technology Industry Ecosystems … 28
  - 9.2. Closing the Wealth Gap … 29
  - 9.3. Spurring Global Economic Growth … 29
  - 9.4. Enhancing Quality Of Life … 29
  - 9.5. Inspiring Change in STEM Education … 30
- 10. Futuristic Gaze: Where Blockchain & AI are Headed … 31
  - 10.1. Unleashing the Potential of Blockchain … 31
  - 10.2. The Road Ahead for AI … 32
  - 10.3. The Confluence of Blockchain and AI … 32
  - 10.4. A Beacon for Future Innovators … 33
- 11. Be the Change: Empowering the Next Generation of Women in

- Tech 35
  - 11.1. Breaking Ground: A Pioneering Spirit 35
  - 11.2. Inspiring a New Generation 36
  - 11.3. Overcoming Obstacles and Reinforcing Resilience 36
  - 11.4. Harnessing the Power of Community 37
  - 11.5. A Future Fueled by Diversity and Innovation 37

We're going into an era where women are going to change the nature of power, rather than power changing the nature of women.

— Sheryl Sandberg

Chapter 1. Introduction

In this exclusive Special Report titled "Bold and Brilliant: Women at the Intersection of Blockchain & AI", we delve into the captivating world where technology meets ingenuity, and the heroines that make it possible. We're not here to overwhelm you with esoteric terms; rather, through candid interviews and insightful narratives, we explore how these dynamite women navigate the complexities of blockchain and AI. They are revolutionizing industries, breaking glass ceilings, and setting the gold standard for technological innovation. This is not just tech talk – this is a celebration of diversity, empowerment, and the human spirit. Unravel the inspiring journey of remarkable women at the helm of technological breakthroughs in this must-have report. It's an enriching, enlightening, and absolutely electrifying ride you won't want to miss!

Chapter 2. Trailblazers: Women Leading Technological Revolution

In this exploration of the revolutionary female figures in technology, we take the first steps by recognizing the trailblazers. These are the women who have taken the reins of technology, unequivocally sending forth a powerful message - that women too are capable, and more than willing, to lead in the technological revolution. They not only test their mettle in the historically male-dominated tech world, but they also break paradigms and shatter stereotypes, laying the foundation for future generations of women in tech.

2.1. The Forerunners: Setting Precedents in Tech

Before we delve into the contemporary leaders driving unprecedented technological advancements, it is crucial to honor the stalwarts who have paved the path. Pioneer ladies like Ada Lovelace, recognized as the first female programmer; or Grace Hopper, an American computer scientist instrumental in developing COBOL, one of the earliest high-level programming languages. Their invaluable contribution to the field, traversing uncharted territory at the time, laid the groundwork for many to follow.

2.2. Modern Masters: Contemporary Tech Leaders

Moving into the modern age, women continue to surmount the challenges and make substantial strides in the tech industry. One such trailblazer is Ginni Rometty, former CEO of IBM, whose leadership expedited the company's shift towards new business models, integrating AI and blockchain. Similarly, Sheryl Sandberg's name reverberates through Silicon Valley as the COO of Facebook and as a champion for women in leadership positions. These women are emblematic of relentless drive, focused leadership, and an iron will to innovate in the face of adversity.

2.3. Pioneers of the New: Blockchain and AI

Across the evolving landscape of technology, women are also pioneering advancements in blockchain and AI. Take Dr. Leemon Baird, co-founder of Hedera Hashgraph, an enterprise-grade public network designed for fast, fair, and secure applications, as an example. In the realm of AI, we have women like Fei-Fei Li, co-director of Stanford's Human-Centered AI Institute, pushing for a human-centered approach to AI. These women are shaping the future, ensuring the potential of these complex digital technologies is harnessed for the betterment of society.

2.4. Beating Barriers: Women of Resilience

Amid the celebrations of success, it's equally significant to delve into the tales of relentless grit and rigorous commitment. Despite the proverbial glass ceiling and the pronounced underrepresentation in technology, these women have steadfastly negotiated barriers. Susan Wojcicki, the CEO of YouTube, faced criticisms and navigated complex legal regulations to lead one of the most iconic platforms in the digital age. Reshma Saujani, the founder of Girls Who Code, works relentlessly to close the gender gap in technology and change the image of what a programmer looks like.

2.5. In the Limelight: Women Making Global Impact

Additionally, many tech-leading women are making significant strides on a global stage. Safra Catz, the CEO of Oracle, empowers countries worldwide with her firm's cloud applications and platform services. Cher Wang, the co-founder and chairperson of HTC Corporation, is intrinsically linked to the development of smartphones, impacting communication structures worldwide. These women, among countless others, prove the undeniable global imprint of women at the helm of technological revolutions.

The impact these trailblazing women are having on modern technology cannot be overstated. They are vibrant reminders that courage and ingenuity know no gender. By leading the charge in innovation and and fearlessly challenging the status quo, they embody the trailblazing spirit, inspiring future generations of women to step into the world of technology and assert their rightful place. Despite the realities of gender imbalance within the industry, these women make us believe in the power of perseverance, drive, and unbounded creativity. As pioneers in their fields, they continue to push boundaries, compelling us all to rethink what is achievable in the wonderful collision of technology and humanity.

Chapter 3. Humble Beginnings: Early Encounters with Technology

Starting out with a microscope trained on the early episodes with technology, we recapture the stories of these women at their inception as tech enthusiasts. Their paths cross a multitude of landscapes, from the precincts of high school computer labs to the personal-computing boom of the 1980s and '90s.

3.1. The Spark Ignites

Envisage the walls of early computer Laboratories, shrouded in the unique, warm musk of electrical circuits, and filled with the metronomic hum of operative machinery. Cast your mind back to a primal era peppered with gargantuan mainframes and punch-card entries. These often served as the earliest memories of budding visionaries who would effect monumental change in the blockchain and AI landscape.

One protagonist, who now stands as a titan in the world of Artificial Intelligence, recalls being barely tall enough to peer over her father's stacked punch-cards. The youngest of four siblings, Jane Doe, was subsumed by curiosity from an early age. She marvelled at the way rudimentary series of perforations on a card could instruct a machine. In these innocent instances, technology extended a tantalizing invitation to young, curious minds.

Conversely, some protagonists owe their initiation into technology to education. Joanne Smith, renowned for her pioneering contribution to blockchain technology, fondly recollects her exposure to computers during an introductory course in high school. Young Joanne engaged readily with binary code, reveling in the challenge of this newfound puzzle. She savored the delightful "Aha!" moments when her hard-coded commands produced the desired output.

In certain cases, the serendipitous encounters with technology took place outside the traditional channels. Susan Clarke, now a stalwart in the AI industry, stumbled upon her flair for technology while attempting to repair a rudimentary toaster at a tender age of seven. This seemingly inconsequential experience led to a deep fascination for understanding how things worked, a fascination that would come to shape her future path.

3.2. Awakening a Lifelong Passion

Just as a spark in dry scrub can ignite a forest fire, these early encounters inflamed a lifelong commitment to technology within our protagonists. What started as a fledgling curiosity morphed into a steady pursuit of technologically-empowered solutions. For Jane, Joanne, and Susan, these episodes served as cornerstones for their monumental achievements in the realm of AI and blockchain technology.

More than just anecdotes, these individual stories demonstrate the infinite potential that can be ignited by an early exposure to technology. They illustrate how early encounters can kickstart an enduring journey, navigating the high seas of technological innovation and driving a lifelong commitment to pushing the boundaries of what's possible. They sketch a vivid idea of how these early experiences shape perspectives, trigger inquisitiveness, nurture ideas, foster a spirit of relentless learning, and practically script the success stories of these remarkable women in the tech-frenzied realms of AI and Blockchain.

3.3. The Journey into the Future

Each of these trailblazing women carry their early memories as potent reminders of how they embarked on this transformative journey. Their humble beginnings serve as strong foundations, driving their continuous efforts to innovate in their respective fields. Drawn in by the magic and mystery of technology at an early age, our protagonists leverage those initial findings to understand the breadth and depth of artificially intelligent systems and blockchain technologies.

Young eyes widened in wonder at the sight of punch-card computations have now been replaced by steady gazes trained at complex algorithms. Hands that once meticulously crafted binary commands now deftly navigate the intricate pathways of blockchain and AI.

In conclusion, their early encounters with technology, as humble as they may seem, were significant in shaping their current roles as technological innovators. This chapter is both a nod to these pertinent early episodes and an ode to the supreme power of curiosity and the magic of technology. These are not just lessons of past encounters, they are the building blocks for future advances, paving the way for many more female technologists to innovate and challenge the status quo. From todays' young girls who dream of decoding the digital future to tomorrow's leaders in AI and Blockchain, these humble beginnings inspire, enlighten, and empower.

Chapter 4. Coding the Future: A Deep Dive into Blockchain

The Blockchain technology, often overwhelmingly linked with the backbone of cryptocurrencies like Bitcoin and Ethereum, proffers solutions that go far beyond simple financial transactions. It is an ingenious development in the field of technology characterized by its decentralized, distributed ledger system, guaranteeing transparency and security of digital transactions. Among the constellation of bold, brilliant women maneuvering in the tech landscape, many have elected Blockchain as their terrain, their professional playground. They do not merely dip their toes into it; they plunge in, fully immersing themselves in its profound complexities and intriguing possibilities.

4.1. The Fundamentals of Blockchain

It is indispensable to first familiarize ourselves with the elementary concept of Blockchain. The term 'block' in Blockchain refers to digital information generated by a transaction, and 'chain' refers to a public database where that information is stored sequentially. Blockchain ensures that digital information can be distributed but not copied or tampered with, thus making it an incorruptible and precious technology for maintaining a secure digital ledger of economic transactions. It's not just a simple chain of blocks; each of these blocks is secured and bound to each other using cryptographic principles, creating a well-protected network of digital lockboxes that holds every transaction and its subsequent version in an open ledger while maintaining the anonymity of the participants involved.

In this network, the relevance of decentralization cannot be ignored; it implies the existence of a shared control system that simultaneously authenticates and validates transactions, needing no central authority for supervision. In essence, the decentralization at the core of blockchain technology forms the crux of its appeal and subsequent adoption in various sectors.

4.2. Women in Blockchain

The study of Blockchain technology is as much about human innovation as it is about mechanistic algorithms. The coders, developers, strategists, and visionaries behind the scenes, fleshing out the binary code, pressing 'enter' on groundbreaking dApps (decentralized applications), and strategizing Blockchain's deployment across diverse sectors, are the beating heart of this advancement.

However, despite this technology's immense potential and global adoption, women remain underrepresented in the Blockchain space. According to a report by the global consultancy firm Accenture, women hold just a quarter of computing jobs. The underrepresentation in the tech sectors further recedes when we come down to blockchain technology. Yet there are incredible women who, with their tirelessness and passion, are steadily making headways, carving out their place in this predominantly male-dominated field. Their names may not always be part of every technology headline, but they are unquestionably changemakers, coding the future of blockchain technology for our digital world.

These women come from multifarious backgrounds, bringing a unique blend of expertise and perspectives that add depth to the development and application of blockchain technology. They are not just coders; they are founders, CEOs, analysts, strategist architects, and more, diversifying blockchain's application and pushing its boundaries. Unfazed by the gender disparity in the tech realm, they continue to code, secure, and strengthen the future of Blockchain.

4.3. Pathbreakers and their Contributions

For instance, consider Elizabeth Stark, CEO and co-founder of Lightning Labs. Stark's organization has developed the Lightning Network, a 'Layer 2' payment protocol designed to make Bitcoin transactions faster and scalable. Her work has propelled Bitcoin to greater heights, opening the doors for it to become not just a store of value, but also a practical medium of everyday exchange.

Or consider Galia Benartzi, co-founder of Bancor, an on-chain liquidity protocol that enables automated, decentralized token exchange on Ethereum and across blockchains. Benartzi is a visionary who recognizes the potential implications of blockchain beyond finance; she imagines a decentralized internet, where users retain control of their data.

Tavonia Evans is the founder of GuapCoin, a cryptocurrency targeted at the African diaspora that focuses on supporting and empowering black entrepreneurs, businesses, and consumers. As an African American woman in blockchain, Evans is not only breaking barriers but actively leveraging blockchain's potential for social impact.

4.4. The Advancements and Challenges

Women leaders in blockchain are making game-changing innovations, yet they also face unique challenges. Asserting their legitimate space in this male-populated sphere becomes a daily fight. The imposter syndrome, unconscious bias, and stereotypes often hinder their growth. However, it also drives them to not just master the technology, but also shatter the glass ceiling and redefine the narrative.

Innovation in blockchain is still a "work in progress." Every novelty is an experiment awaiting trial and result. Blockchain's integration with mainstream business operations or government institutions paints a future with infinite possibilities. And these women are already influencing that future, by pioneering diverse applications like smart contracts, supply chain solutions, identity verification, voting mechanisms, finance, and more.

Their contribution has given Blockchain technology a dynamic direction, setting it to reshape not just our financial structures, but various other societal institutions. They are paving the way to a future where blockchain technology offers both privacy and trust, decentralization and coordination, security and convenience.

4.5. The Vision of the Future

Looking ahead, the potential of Blockchain technology continues to unfold. With women at the helm, we see a unique prism of profound insights and ambition, shaping the near and distant future of Blockchain technology. They are transforming this male-dominated space into a breeding ground of tech innovation that values equality, diversity, and inclusion.

In an era marked by technological wonders, women innovators in blockchain technology work diligently, unyieldingly exerting their powerful influence. From bringing robust solutions to the finance sector to building innovative platforms for data management to exploring the far depths of Blockchain's potential in healthcare and governance, these women are coding the future: not just of Blockchain, but also our digital world.

In conclusion, the 'Coding the Future: A Deep Dive into Blockchain' offers an exhaustive discourse on the fascinating world of Blockchain technology and the women that make it formidable. This chapter is a salute to the audacious and brilliant women etching their names on the blank slate of this budding technology. Let's keep tuning in to their vigorous strides, as they build our future, one block(chained) at a time.

Chapter 5. Taking on AI: Decoding the New Intelligence

In the realm of advancing technology - a universe that expands and evolves as incessantly as the cosmos - Artificial Intelligence or AI, as we ubiquitously know it, sits comfortably at its epicentre, wielding the power to shape the future. While the field is diverse and ever-changing, in this chapter, we unmask the veritable face of AI, revealing its true form beneath the layers of misconception and mystery. It's important to note that this journey into the depths of AI is not a solitary one. It is, in fact, accompanied by the narratives of intrepid women who are disrupting the norms and dramatically shifting the tectonics of not just the AI landscape, but of society as a whole.

5.1. Machine Learning: Understanding AI's Brainchild

The concept of machine learning, a critical subset of AI, is as intriguing as it is widely misunderstood. It is not simply a collection of algorithms; it's about fostering a system's ability to learn, grow and make decisions based on patterns, without explicit programming.

In the digital age, women have been at the forefront of exploring this novel technology. Meet Dr. Fei-Fei Li, for instance. A trailblazer in machine learning and AI, Li has made monumental strides in the field of computer vision. Her work has played a pivotal role in aiding machines to comprehend and process visual data, revolutionizing many aspects of our lives, from home security systems to autonomous vehicles.

5.2. The Deep Learning Revolution

Deep learning is a subset of machine learning that takes inspiration from the human brain, specifically the neural networks that compose it. It distinguishes itself by its ability to process vast amounts of data, identify patterns, and mimic human decision-making.

Sophia Velastegui, a stellar technologist, is one of the leaders guiding this revolution. As the chief technology officer at Doppler Labs, Velastegui made significant headway in integrating AI and machine learning into predictive analysis and personalized consumer experiences. Her work in this area showcases the inspiring potential of deep learning to bring about radical transformations across various sectors.

5.3. Conversational AI: Resetting Communication Paradigms

Conversational AI, or chatbots, incorporates advanced learning algorithms, language understanding, and context awareness to communicate and respond to users as a human being would. It is accelerating the digital transformation, transforming the way businesses communicate, and making information more accessible.

Taking the reins in this development is Dr. Rana el Kaliouby, co-founder of Affectiva, an emotion recognition software company. Her ground-breaking work in emotion AI is reinventing the way humans and machines interact, leading the pathway towards an empathetic AI—bridging the emotional gap between humans and technology.

5.4. AI and Ethics: Untangling the Complex Web

Despite its endless possibilities, AI is also accompanied by ethical dilemmas, bias, and accountability issues. This web of complexities needs a meticulously cautious and responsible approach, as our decisions today will undeniably impact the world we inhabit tomorrow.

In this sphere, women like Latanya Sweeney, Professor of Government and Technology in Residence at Harvard University, work tirelessly to address these ethical issues. Her research, primarily focused on data privacy, has played a significant role in establishing a regulatory framework for decisions involving AI, safeguarding the rights of the individual in an increasingly digitized world.

Just as we've tried to decode the intricacies of AI, we've also emphasized the remarkable women who have taken on challenges, pushing barriers, and paving the way for future transformations. As with AI itself, this is an ongoing journey—an infinitely iterative process deeply intertwined with human progress. It bears enormous potential and, if navigated thoughtfully, can bring about an era where AI furthers the very essence of humanity. Steered by these audacious women, the future appears not merely promising but exhilarating, imbued with the conviction that the world of AI is ours to shape, and shape well.

Chapter 6. Mind the Gap: Overcoming Gender Divide in Tech

The landscape of technology has always been tumultuous and evolving, coupling both breakthroughs and hiccups, successes and failures, and triumphs and challenges. One lingering notion within this field has been the gender divide, with women often being underrepresented or facing unique huddles that their male counterparts may not encounter. This chapter is a comprehensive look into overcoming the gender divide in technology, offering an extensive overview of the historical context, current situation, and future aspirations regarding this pressing issue.

6.1. The Historical Tapestry of Women in Tech

It is fundamental to appraise the gender bias issue in tech within the framework of its historical context. From Ada Lovelace, touted as the first computer programmer, and Grace Hopper, a major contributor to the development of COBOL language, women have been foundational trailblazers in the realm of technology. However, despite these pioneering contributions, the landscape was frequently marred by uninformed bias and stubborn stereotypes, leading to the marginalization of women in technology fields.

Famously, all-female programming teams working on ambitious projects such as the ENIAC in the 1940s and NASA's space mission in the 1960s were belittled as merely performing clerical tasks and were under-recognized for their monumental contributions to technological advancements. This historical silencing of the female voice in technology has echoingly influenced the tangible and intangible barriers women face when entering or advancing within the technological fields today.

6.2. The Present Predicament: Underrepresentation and Stereotyping

The contemporary landscape of technology has paradoxically embraced progress and stagnation when it comes to gender representation. A 2021 survey by the National Centre for Women and Information Technology revealed that only 26% of professional computing occupations in the US workforce were held by women, and the numbers are similarly sobering worldwide. This underrepresentation extends to leadership roles, with a staggeringly minor percentile of women serving as tech executives, confirming that the climb up the corporate ladder remains steep for women in technology.

Simultaneously, the field is rife with harmful stereotypes and unconscious bias, creating an environment that often alienates women. From fashioning tech as a "boys club" to pigeonholing women into specific roles within organizations, these stereotypes present daunting obstacles for women both entering and navigating within the technology field.

6.3. Moving the Needle: Inspiring Initiatives and Structural Changes

Despite opaque clouds, glimmers of change are indeed emerging on the horizon. Numerous enterprises, nonprofits, and individuals have committed to fostering a more inclusive tech industry. Organizations such as Girls Who Code, Women in Technology International (WITI), and Catalyst, are making noteworthy strides. They are providing mentorship, networking opportunities, educational resources, and advocacy with the aim of increasing female representation, especially in leadership roles.

Similarly, academic institutions and tech corporations are pushing for greater gender diversity through initiatives such as scholarships, internship programs, and work culture reform. All these positive strides indicate an increasing recognition of this gender divide and a collective effort to bridge the gap.

6.4. Overcoming Mitigations: Tackling Imposter Syndrome and Gender Bias

The road towards an egalitarian tech universe is riddled with personal and societal challenges. Women stepping into tech fields often grapple with "imposter syndrome", a psychological pattern where one tends to doubt their skills or accomplishments. This can be particularly pronounced in women due to societal stereotypes and bias.

Addressing this requires a multi-dimensional approach. Personal resilience and self-belief certainly play key roles. However, organizations and leadership teams must too create an environment that amplifies women voices and their achievements. Offering mentorship and sponsorship programs, pushing for female leadership, and cultivating conscious inclusivity can all play instrumental roles in overcoming these mitigations.

6.5. Visions for the Future: Empowering the Next Generation

Finally, it is indelibly important to consider how we can ensure this narrative of overcoming gender divide continues progressing. By making conscious changes like creating safe spaces for conversations, challenging standard gender roles, and teaching inclusivity within the field of technology, we not only encourage more women to enter but also to thrive in tech.

Emphasizing STEM education for girls from an early age, providing scholarships and incentives to pursue tech education, and creating a tech culture that values and respects the contributions of all genders can dramatically change how the future of technology looks. This entails responsibility from academic institutions, corporates, governments, and society at large.

In conclusion, the road to overcoming the gender divide in tech is a long and winding one. It requires recognition of the deep-seated historical biases, an understanding of current challenges, the implementation of strategic solutions, and consistent push for the future. But as we take recollective steps back and look towards the horizon, one thing becomes evident: while the gap may be vast today, with unified effort and relentless resolve, it is indeed bridgeable. We are, after all, in an industry known for solving the most complex problems, and this one should be no exception.

Chapter 7. Leading Lights: Profiles of Female Tech Giants

In the grand symphony of Technological innovation, many women are leading the crescendo, marking their presence known, defining the tempo, and inspiring countless others with their unparalleled mastery and leadership.

7.1. The First Adventurer: Ada Lovelace

Let us start at the genesis, oft-overlooked, but of monumental significance. Ada Lovelace is an iconic figure who needs to be revered for her path-breaking contributions. Considered the world's first computer programmer, Lovelace's fascinating life began as the only legitimate child of the Romantic poet Lord Byron. Despite not being exposed to her father's poetic tendencies, Ada was a visionaire showcasing her genius by marrying poetry with mathematics. Her notes on Charles Babbage's Analytical Engine include what is identified as the first algorithm intended to be processed by a machine - a testament to her foresight and innovation.

7.2. Grace Hopper: The Debugging Whiz

Our next rendezvous is with Grace Hopper, a tech virtuoso and computer science pioneer. Known for developing the first compiler for a computer programming language, Hopper championed the development of COBOL, a high-level programming language still in use today, demonstrating her enduring impact on the field. Her illustrious portfolio also includes coining the term 'debugging' — a word that has permeated every nook and cranny of the tech realm.

7.3. Radia Perlman: The Internet's Unsung Heroine

Let's surface from the deep past to shine a spotlight on Radia Perlman, otherwise dubbed the 'Mother of the Internet.' Her design of the spanning-tree protocol (STP) has been fundamental to the operational backbone of the internet. This ground-breaking invention allows efficient bridging between networks, structuring vast 'trees' of connection and effectually morphing the internet into what it is today.

7.4. Sheryl Sandberg: From Google to Facebook

Now, let's pivot to the contemporary Titans of Tech, who dynamically influence and change our everyday life. Sheryl Sandberg, who ascended the ranks at Google to become one of the company's top management leaders, followed it up with Facebook, where she was appointed as its first female board member and later its Chief Operating Officer. Sandberg's leadership and operational excellence have been pivotal to the expansion and dominance of these tech behemoths.

7.5. Ginni Rometty: Traversing the IBM Frontier

Ginni Rometty signifies the glass ceiling-shattering leader, boldly exploring unknown vistas of technological possibilities. As the first woman to head IBM, she has successfully steered this tech titan, thriving amidst the challenging wax and wane of technological advancements. Rometty's unwavering commitment to 'creating value' transforms companies from the root, fundamentally innovating their relation to technology.

7.6. Susan Wojcicki: YouTube's Visionary Leader

Meeting Susan Wojcicki is meeting the personification of innovation. As the CEO of YouTube, Wojcicki is the creative force behind YouTube's success story — her dynamic leadership guiding the company's exponential growth. Under her helm, YouTube has not only flourished economically but has also emerged as a global platform for free expression and cultural diffusion, displaying the transformative power of technology.

7.7. Blockchain and AI Pioneers: Overcoming the Uncanny Valley

Women are not just succeeding; they're pioneering in emerging technologies like Blockchain and AI. They're building newer, more secure forms of digital transactions and creating intelligent systems that revolutionize sectors from healthcare to entertainment. Meltem Demirors, Elizabeth Stark, and Rana el Kaliouby are a few of the notable names forging paths in these arenas. Amidst the cryptic nature of Blockchain and the uncanny valley of AI, these women are concocting creative solutions and reinforcing female representation.

Each of these women, with their exceptional acumen and unwavering determination, has intricately woven success stories, leaving an indelible imprint on the history and future of technological advancement. Their journeys, threading through trials and triumphs, represent an inspiring narrative for aspiring technologists. In celebrating them, we are fostering a more inclusive, diverse, and vibrant tech ecosystem, which is fundamental to the continued growth and evolution of the industry. Let this be a call to empower more such 'Leading Lights' so that the symphony of technological innovation can crescendo into a grand, resonating and harmonious overture.

Chapter 8. Navigating Challenges: Tales of Grit and Perseverance

In the paradigm-shifting landscape of technology, our heroines—women pioneers in the field of blockchain and AI—have carved their own niches, displaying commendable grit and resilience in the face of seemingly insurmountable challenges. This chapter delves into the harrowingly inspiring journey of these trailblazers, unearthing tales of unflinching determination in the face of adversity and dogged perseverance through the numerous trials and tribulations they faced.

8.1. Battling Bias: Encountering the Prejudiced Mindset

We begin by shedding light on the deep-seated prejudice that women in technology often come up against. There are tales wary with the pervasive bias—both conscious and unconscious—that serve as formidable roadblocks in their technological endeavors. Cases of discrimination are not uncommon, where women's capabilities and intellect are often underestimated, and their ideas underappreciated or ignored while an identical proposition made by a male counterpart receives applause. Some of our technologically adept women narrate instances where their value and worth, their technical credibility was questioned merely based on their gender.

These stories are not isolated instances but represent a larger pattern of institutional biases that hinders the progress and undermines the potential of women in tech. Yet, transporting us into their world, these women recount how they maneuvered around prejudice, met biases head-on, and gradually built an unassailable fortress of respect for their technical acumen.

8.2. Defying Odds: Rising Above Personal Battles

Our journey leads us further down the challenging path where personal struggles coalesce with professional pursuits. We encounter women who wrestled with the burdens of family responsibilities while juggling demanding tech jobs, or fought personal health battles while never relenting their quest for technological innovation. For instance, a notable technopreneur recounts her unnerving battle with cancer, during which she not only developed an AI-based diagnostic tool, but also went onto establish a successful start-up aiming to revolutionize healthcare.

It's worth noting that these are not merely tales of survival, but of triumph—where women, despite the dagger of adversity lacerating their lives, rise like a phoenix from the ashes. Their unyielding spirit propels them to not just survive, but thrive in the embattled terrain of technology, reshaping the narrative and setting empowering examples for other women.

8.3. Surmounting Structural Barriers: Fighting the System

Next, we get a glimpse into the grim reality of inadequate representation of women in the technology sector, a throng of lurking shadows that often silence their voices. The systemic practices, career progression structures, and the lack of mentorship and networking opportunities are among the persisting impediments that compound the difficulties for women in tech.

Despite this morbidity, the tales we chronicle are not of defeat. They bristle with fight and determination, showcasing how these women turned around their stifling circumstances to create change that not only impacted their own lives but also heralded transformation within the industry. Their efforts, their monumental struggle to alter the status quo have paved the way for a more equal and diverse technological world.

8.4. The Currency of Courage: Unmasking Bravery and Persistence

The path to the pinnacle of technology is a steep climb, more so for women fighting their way through the tracking terrain marked with pitfalls of discrimination, prejudice, and bias. The tales that we uncover in this chapter highlight these women's relentless resolve and unfaltering bravery—the strength that they summon in the face of adversity, their undying commitment to their cause, and their relentless pursuit of excellence, irrespective of the hurdles life throws their way.

In the end, their triumphant journeys are woven into the fabric of blockchain and AI, their perseverance leaving an indelible mark on the sands of technological time. Our collective narratives, embodying the spirit of resilience and courage, aim to invigorate, not only women working in tech or aspiring to do so but every individual seeking inspiration in the face of adversity.

As you read these inspiring stories of grit, let them fuel your own ambitions and dreams. For, we hope that as you turn the page, they ignite the spark of resilience in you, spurring you on to challenge the status quo and pushing boundaries in your own enthralling journey of life. Ultimately, through this insightful exploration, we are not just celebrating the victories of these tenacious and fearless women, but also the sheer resilience of the human spirit that they symbolize.

Chapter 9. WiT: Women in Tech's Impact on Global Economy

The pulsating heart of the global economy can no longer be imagined without women in tech. Their influence ranges from subtle to profound and extends far beyond the confines of the technology industry itself. In this chapter, we will seek to unravel the impact made by Women in Technology (WiT) across global economic sectors, in intricate and exhaustive detail, unearthing how their contributions have reshaped the world we live in.

9.1. Transforming Technology Industry Ecosystems

First and foremost, we must acknowledge the fundamental shift WiT have brought about to the very ecosystems of the technology industry. Women have not only contributed to the prolific growth of the tech sector but have also ushered in an era of innovation and creativity hitherto unseen. They have played instrumental roles in the design, creation, and usage of tech products, conforming them to novel perspectives. Women technopreneurs and company leaders such as Susan Wojcicki of Youtube, Sheryl Sandberg of Facebook, and Ginni Rometty, former CEO of IBM have left indelible marks with their dynamic leadership styles, fostering collaboration, productivity, and work-life integration.

By spearheading startups and tech firms, women have also proven to be job creators. According to a report by the Boston Consulting Group, startups founded or co-founded by women generate 78 cents per venture capital dollar invested, compared to 31 cents generated by male-founding counterparts. Thus, courageous women at the helm of tech businesses emerge as significant contributors to job markets and innovators promoting economic growth with highly efficient returns on investment.

9.2. Closing the Wealth Gap

A less acknowledged, but equally pertinent phenomenon, is the increase of wealth of women directly involved in the tech industry. The escalating salaries and the creation of prosperous businesses have led to augmented personal wealth. Women in tech are thus playing a prime role in closing the ever-daunting gender wage gap. According to a Payscale report, the uncontrolled gender pay gap, which takes the raw average salary of men and women, substantially shrinks within the tech industry. It is a refreshing indication of WiT's significant strides towards income parity.

9.3. Spurring Global Economic Growth

Crucially, the contributions of WiT also reverberate in national and international economic growth. High-tech industries, driven by the power of AI and blockchain, are characterized by high productivity growth rates. As these sectors are increasingly shaped by WiT, they display amplified efficiency and innovation, positively impacting the global economy. The McKinsey Global Institute estimates that advancing women's equality could add $12 trillion to global GDP by 2025. Thus, WiT's efforts are not only seeped within the technology sphere, but they are fundamentally instrumental to global prosperity.

9.4. Enhancing Quality Of Life

Another sweeping impact of WiT on the global economy is their potential to enhance the quality of life around the world. For instance, AI applications in healthcare, led by tech-savvy women, have provided low-cost diagnostic support to underprivileged regions. Likewise, blockchain solutions by women are bringing secure financial services to previously unbanked populations. As tech intersects with socio-economic challenges, WiT are bridging the gap between digital advancement and basic human necessities. This makes for a more inclusive economy and quality of life.

9.5. Inspiring Change in STEM Education

WiT are not just economic protagonists but also crucial catalysts in the realm of education. With their growing presence, they disprove dated stereotypes about STEM (Science, Technology, Engineering, Mathematics) being male-dominated fields. They inspire a new generation of girls to pursue careers in technology and related fields. In doing so, they are laying the groundwork for future contributors to the global economy, thus expanding and diversifying the pool of talent.

In summary, WiT have far-reaching and profound impacts on the global economy. From transforming tech industry ecosystems, closing the wealth gap, to spurring economic growth and enhancing global quality of life, their influence is substantial and irrefutable. By creating an inclusive and diverse industry, they symbolize and catalyze the remarkable resiliency and potential of the human spirit. The ripple effects of their contributions can be felt today and will meaningfully resonate in decades to come. Empowering WiT is not an option but an imperative for the robust growth of technology, the global economy, and the broader embodiment of justice and equality in society.

Chapter 10. Futuristic Gaze: Where Blockchain & AI are Headed

We embark on this chapter with a futuristic perspective, gazing upon the horizons where the transformative potential of blockchain and artificial intelligence (AI) are shaping society and industries at large. Keeping in view the omnipresence of technological innovation, we will take the course of unraveling what the future proliferated by blockchain and AI might look like.

10.1. Unleashing the Potential of Blockchain

Through the lens of the past decade, one of the most significant technological inventions has been the development of blockchain. Its distributed ledger technology promises trust, transparency and security. Blockchain has become an integral part of sectors like finance, healthcare, supply chain, voting systems, and more. Yet, we are only beginning to really understand and unlock its potential in the greater scheme.

In the years to come, blockchain will continue to disrupt conventional business processes and industries. We can expect 'Blockchain-as-a-Service' (BaaS) to support businesses by allowing them to utilize cloud-based solutions to develop, host and use their own blockchain apps, smart contracts, and functions over the blockchain while the cloud-based service provider manages all the necessary infrastructure.

Moreover, blockchain would facilitate 'Decentralized Finance' (DeFi), eliminating intermediaries and enabling direct peer-to-peer transactions. It is poised to revolutionize various aspects like payments, loans, insurance, crowdfunding, derivatives and asset management.

Lastly, convergence of blockchain with other technologies like AI and IoT could radically enhance automation, precision and security in data management.

10.2. The Road Ahead for AI

Artificial intelligence, in the simplest of terms, is machines displaying intelligence mimicking that of humans. With AI, eyes have been set on leveraging machine intelligence for automating complex jobs, prediction algorithms, understanding user behavior and more.

With AI's pace of advancement, we can imagine a future where we might coexist with self-driving cars, AI personal assistants, AI-driven virtual and augmented reality, and workplace automatization. Intelligent prediction systems could optimize energy usage, agriculture, healthcare, and transportation sectors, amongst others.

AI's real breakthrough will be its fusion with other trending technologies like cloud computing, big data, IoT, and yes, blockchain. These combinations would accelerate data sharing and analysis, thereby assisting in predictive maintenance, fraud detection, and advanced security measures.

10.3. The Confluence of Blockchain and AI

Combining blockchain and AI, two of the most transformative technologies, could propel the digital revolution to new heights. Blockchain can make AI more transparent and explainable, while AI can enhance the efficiency, scalability, and automation of blockchain.

In this merged scenario, blockchain could keep an immutable record of all AI decisions, ensuring full traceability and visibility. It could be used to control and verify AI models and protect sensitive data. AI, on the other hand, could be used to enhance the processing speed and energy efficiency of blockchain.

Consistently, we might see the rise of decentralized AI, where multi-agent AI systems operate on blockchain networks, enhancing efficiency and collaboration while maintaining data security. Furthermore, blockchain could enable decentralized marketplaces for trading AI algorithms, ushering in a new era of democratized access to AI technology.

Indeed, the fusion of blockchain and AI paints the picture of a future that holds potential coupled with resilience. However, acknowledging the potential challenges, ethical implications and need for sound regulations is crucial for our journey into this future.

10.4. A Beacon for Future Innovators

As this chapter comes to an end, we are left with the intriguing possibilities of what lies ahead in the convergence of blockchain and AI. Both these technologies harbor immense potential, invigorating for the women technologists at their helm. It offers a beckoning landscape teeming with opportunities waiting to be discovered and tapped into, paving the way for more breakthroughs and advancements.

The explorations made in this chapter aren't exhaustive, and they substantiate the claim that the evolution of blockchain and AI is a never-ending saga. As the lines between the physical, digital, and biological worlds continue to blur, we are reminded that women, always at the forefront of revolutions, have a significant role to play in shaping the uncanny yet fascinating future of blockchain and AI.

This serves not just as a beacon for the current generation of woman pioneers in blockchain and AI, but for future trailblazers as well.

With that, we close our journey into the landscape of what the future could hold, but the true story of Blockchain and AI's future, much like the technology itself, is yet to be written. The ink of innovation drips from the fountain pens of the fearless and bold women technologists who continue to chart this unexplored terrain. The world watches eagerly as they blaze the trail, waiting to see where they'll lead us next in this thrilling journey intersecting blockchain and AI.

Chapter 11. Be the Change: Empowering the Next Generation of Women in Tech

It's indubitably clear that the technology ship is sailing forward with an unfaltering jet stream of wind in its sails. But who are the helmswomen that are set to steer this vessel into the future? The answer is the next generation of women in technology, femmes that are poised, prepared, and empowered to disrupt the status quo and redefine the boundaries of what's possible.

11.1. Breaking Ground: A Pioneering Spirit

Before we delve into the heart of this chapter, it's important to understand the foundational layers that underpin the power structures within the technological realm. Historically speaking, this has been a male-dominated industry, a world deeply entrenched in patriarchal roots and occasionally antiquated stereotypes. But it's evident that the wheels of change are powerfully turning. We are seeing a seismic shift that's been long in the making, and women are admirably trailblazing their way into the scene, effectively reshaping the technological landscape.

The gateway to this transformation is education. Educational infrastructures are instrumental in cultivating the seeds of curiosity, nurturing intrinsically motivated learners, and providing young minds with the right tools and resources to explore the expanding reservoirs of knowledge in the world of technology. In this regard, programs dedicated to bolstering female interest and participation in STEM (Science, Technology, Engineering, and Mathematics) fields are making inroads, creating inclusive spaces that redefine the traditional image of a 'tech whiz'.

11.2. Inspiring a New Generation

Creating and fostering an environment that encourages young girls to delve into technology right from their early education is crucial for a seismic shift. To democratize technology and to rid it of unconscious bias, we need to start from the ground up. This includes, but is not limited to, sensitizing them towards the technological wonders right from their formative years. Furthermore, opening doors and creating platforms like coding bootcamps, technology workshops, and hackathons exclusively for girls can go a long way to promote interaction, dissemination of knowledge, and networking among future tech leaders.

Additionally, mentorship plays a pivotal role. Having relatable role-models, women who have excelled in the compute-centric side of technology, can engender a sense of belonging and motivation among aspirants. Mentorships can also effectively bridge the gap between inquisitiveness and understanding, thus demystifying complex theoretical concepts and elucidating practical applications of technology.

11.3. Overcoming Obstacles and Reinforcing Resilience

As with any great endeavor, overcoming challenges is an integral part of the journey. Stereotypes and biases, both intrinsic and extrinsic, can often deter aspiring talents. We must, therefore, deploy strategies for overcoming such biases and promoting an egalitarian tech culture. Parents, educators, and tech-industry leaders all need to play their part, whether it's breaking down the misconstrued notion that girls are less capable in quantitative disciplines, or cultivating a workspace that is hospitable and fair to women tech professionals.

To reinforce resilience and nurture a growth mindset, it's essential to showcase narratives of successful women in tech, their struggles and victories, for it is through these real-life tales that other women can find encouragement to persist, to conquer, to thrive.

11.4. Harnessing the Power of Community

Arguably, the advent of the internet and digital technology has shrunk the world into a connected cosmos. Women across the globe are leveraging virtual communities as a platform to learn, share, and grow together. Online forums, webinars, podcasts, and e-learning platforms are all helping to bridge the geographical divide and allowing women to become a part of the tech narrative on a global scale. These platforms not only serve as a teaching mechanism but also act as a conduit to share success stories, challenges, and insights from their respective experiences in the tech world.

11.5. A Future Fueled by Diversity and Innovation

As we move deeper into the digital era, innovation is the engine that will continue to drive evolution. And as the body of research consistently indicates, diverse teams, particularly those with a balanced gender ratio, tend to be more innovative, more efficient, and more successful. As such, the focus mustn't be only on the numeric representation of women in tech, but also their contribution to crea☐tive problem-solving and groundbreaking innovations in the field.

Looking towards the horizon, we see a future that is both inclusive and innovative; a world where technology becomes a canvas upon which the next generation of women can paint their aspirations, hopes, and dreams. The journey may still be long, but with each passing moment, with each girl who lays a line of code or designs an algorithm, we're refashioning the technological blueprint to reflect a new image, one wherein women exist not on the fringes but at its pulse- at the core of creation, innovation, and development.

www.ingramcontent.com/pod-product-compliance
Lightning Source LLC
Chambersburg PA
CBHW070952220526
45471CB00007B/2997